QUANTUM PRAYER
LEAP
DECREES

THE DECADE OF DESTINY

I0151534

SARAH MORGAN

ISBN: 978-1-5136-5881-0

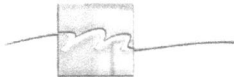

MORGAN PUBLISHING
The Pen of a Ready Writer

Quantum Prayer Leap Decrees

Published by Morgan Publishing
888-320-5622

Join the Movement, and Connect with us on:
www.prayeracademy.university
www.prayeracademyglobal.com
www.facebook.com/prayeracademyglobal
www.instagram.com/prayeracademyglobal
www.twitter.com/prayeracademy

DEDICATION

This series of books is dedicated to the thousands of Prayer Academy Students across this nation, the Prayer Altar Call family, and the countless elite warriors, intercessors, travailing women, and warring men. The Bible says, *"The generous will prosper; those who refresh others will themselves be refreshed" (Proverbs 11:25, NIV).* As you have energized, restored, and revived others through your intercession, may you experience a wind of refreshing blowing over you in the place of PRAYER— the place of POWER!

Yours Truly,
Sarah Morgan

CONTENTS

ACKNOWLEDGMENTS

First, to my Abba Father, Pater, Provider, Protector, Preserver, to His Son Jesus and to precious Holy Spirit, my Senior Partner, without this Terrific Trio, I can do nothing. I am eternally grateful and privileged to serve and committed to the cause.

Karla Allen, thank you for editing, formatting, proofing, and helping expedite the process of production. You are a blessing to your generation. I appreciate you.

Sarah Morgan

PREFACE

HOW TO USE THIS BOOK

The Prayer Declaration Series is designed to strengthen your relationship with God by gaining an awareness of the importance of engaging in prayer for tangible results.

Effective prayer will cause you to soar like an eagle in God's plan for your life. It is a vital key to tapping into the wisdom of God, which will elevate you above mediocrity to produce astounding exploits to the Glory of God.

"But the people who know their God shall prove themselves strong and shall stand firm and do exploits [for God]" (Daniel 11:32).

An intimate prayer life will stabilize and secure every area of your life. Contrary to some opinions, prayer should not be boring. Prayer should be the highlight of your day. Albeit, there is no set way to pray; there are guidelines:

1. Pray to God, the Father, in the name of Jesus Christ.
2. Seek to Establish a Good Personal Relationship with the Lord.
3. Make Sure Your Prayers Always Line Up With the Perfect Will of God for Your Life.
4. Back-Up Your Prayers with Specific Scripture Verses.
5. Do not be Afraid to Write Your Prayers Out to the Lord.
6. Do not be Afraid to go into *Prevailing* Prayer, as Lead by the Holy Spirit.
7. Ask the Holy Spirit to Help You with Your Prayer Life (Romans 8:26).
8. Ask Others to Pray in Agreement with You When Needed.
9. Always Include Prayers of Thanksgiving.
10. Start with Early Morning Prayer and Keep an Ear Tuned to the Holy Spirit Throughout the Entire Day.
11. Read and use the Prayers/Confessions found in the Prayer Declaration Series.
12. Pray in the Holy Spirit. If You have Received the Gift of the Holy Spirit (the language of the Spirit),

you can receive it today. If You Have not received Him, ask; He will fill you. The Gift is Free!

13. Confess Scriptures Straight from the Word.

14. Pray a Scripture from the Word and Expand upon that Prayer, Spontaneously.

15. Pray the Word that is Hidden/Planted in your Heart, Spontaneously.

16. Receive Specific Guidance from the Holy Spirit as to What and How to Pray the Word.

17. Meditate on What You Read From Scripture and Pray the Word from Memory.

18. Pray God's Word and in Your Heavenly Language, and Alternate as the Spirit Leads.

Finally, have a great hunger for God—desperation to pray His will and submit to Him from your heart/spirit. Allow the Holy Spirit to search you. Then, be diligent in crucifying your flesh. Do not be satisfied with self-directed prayer; dig deep into the spirit realm.

When you allow the Holy Spirit to lead you, your spirit will issue, out the forces of life, with effectual fervent prayer. Continue to press into the spirit realm, until your spiritual antennas' tune in to the promptings and leadings of the Holy Spirit. Then as you speak, every stronghold is destroyed, and the power of God released.

When you press into the place of prayer, in the spirit, your spirit becomes one with the Spirit of God. Then, you will pray His desires from your heart, and become intimate with Him, commune with Him, and become lost in Him. It is at that moment; your mind is in total subjection to pray the will of the Father.

Prayer is not forceful but flowing. Prayer is such a great joy that you cannot get enough. May the Spirit of Grace and Supplication fill you to overflowing in the *place of prayer*.

HOW TO ENTER INTO A TIME OF PRAYER

A.C.T

A - Acknowledge Him for Who He is.

"Know ye that the LORD He is God: it is He that hath made us, and not we ourselves; we are His people, and the sheep of His pasture" (Psalms 100:3).

C – Confess Your Sins, Faults, and Shortcomings.

"If we say that we have no sin, we deceive ourselves, and the truth is not in us. If we confess our sins, he is faithful and just to forgive us our sins, and to cleanse us from all unrighteousness" (1 John 1:8-9).

T - Thanksgiving

"Enter into his gates with thanksgiving, and into his courts with praise be thankful unto him, and bless his name" (Psalms 100:4).

QUANTUM LEAP PRAYER DECREES

INTRODUCTION

QUANTUM PRAYER LEAP INTO THE NEXT DECADE OF DESTINY

A Quantum Leap is a sudden, highly significant advance. It's a breakthrough, sudden substantial increase, or advance. "This may ensure success, and it will represent a quantum leap from where you were to where you are supposed to be in your life and destiny. Through Prayer Quantum Leap Decrees, you will rise in rank and status.

> *"**Thou shalt also Decree a thing, and it shall be established unto thee:** and the light shall shine upon thy ways. When men are cast down, then thou shalt say, **There is lifting up;** and he shall save the humble person" (Job 22:28-29).*

> *"And from Jesus Christ, who is the faithful witness, and the first begotten of the dead, and the prince of the kings of the earth. Unto him*

*that loved us and washed us from our sins in his own blood, **And hath made us kings and priests unto God and his Father;** to him be glory and dominion for ever and ever. Amen"* *(Revelations 1:5-6).*

This scripture qualifies you to make a Decree as a child of God who has been made a king and priest unto God and the Father of our Lord Jesus Christ. Kings are not beggars; kings are in command of their territory, kings are decision-makers and destiny determinants.

The Definition for *Decree*

1. The word decree comes from the French/Latin, meaning a decision with the definition stating that it's "An authoritative order having the force of law."

When you decree, you must first make a decision that change is inevitable, and then use your kingdom authority to bring the earth realm under the force of the law of the power God!

The Definition for *Declare*

1. Declare to make known or state clearly, especially in explicit or formal terms: to declare one's position in a controversy.

2. To announce officially; proclaim: to declare a state of emergency; to declare a winner.

3. To state emphatically to show, reveal, or manifest: the heavens declare the glory of God.

"Thou shalt also decree a thing, and it shall be established unto thee: and the light shall shine upon thy ways."
Job 22:28

The person making the decree must be in a position of power and authority to do so. You have the power and authority as a king and priest to make a decree and expect that they will be carried out.

You shall decree. The power is yours, state your case and write out the conditions regarding your home, family, ministry, and all that concern you. The words that you speak will be established, that means it will be manifested, revealed, and shown to be true, as you have spoken it.

The light shall shine upon thy way means there will be enlightenment in your mind, and spirit that will cause you to see the path that is laid before you. You will not stumble about in darkness, walk timidly, and unsure but will have clarity, purpose, and direction.

Therefore, you have the power, the authority to speak out a thing in your life, and expect to see it manifested in the reality of your world.

What you decree you should also declare that is to speak emphatically, make known and clearly state your position upon the matter. To both decree and declare a thing and expect to see the manifestation, you must know the word of God, so you understand your legal right to have your decree upheld. There are always conditions that you must meet to have the authority to do anything in the kingdom of God.

> *"And it shall come to pass, if thou shalt hearken diligently unto the voice of the LORD thy God, to observe and to do all his commandments which I command thee this day, that the LORD thy God will set thee on high above all nations of the earth"(Deuteronomy 28:1).*

When you hear, receive, and obey the word of God, you are given the power to decree the word. The word of God is life, it is quick, and it is powerful. It is truth, it corrects, it enlightens, it heals, it delivers, and it brings visible results. It does not return without accomplishing that which it was sent to do.

The scripture below helps one comprehend the principle behind speaking the word of God.

"Then the LORD put forth his hand, and touched my mouth. And the LORD said unto me, Behold, I have put my words in thy mouth" (Jeremiah 1:9).

In Jeremiah 1:12, he tells Jeremiah that I will quicken or hasten my word to perform it. Read your Bible; ask the Holy Ghost for assistance and guidance as to what you need to decree in your life on behalf of your families, ministries, city, government, and nation. There is a word in the Word of God that holds the answers to your question. You must understand the principle behind decreeing and declaring.

You must meet the condition – read, hear, obey the word, and speak the word. Believe and expect to see the manifestation. Know that you have the right to legislate and cause change to come based on the power and dominion that God has given you. The work is done on your knees in prayer, and the Holy Ghost will reveal to you what to decree and declare. *"Thou shalt also decree a thing, and it shall be **established** unto thee: and the light shall shine upon thy ways." Job 22:28*

The Definition for *Establish*.

1. To set and fix firmly or unalterably, to settle permanently. I will establish my covenant with

him for an everlasting covenant (Genesis17).

2. To found permanently; to erect and fix or settle; as to establish a colony or an empire.

3. To enact or decree by authority and for permanence; to ordain; to appoint; as, to establish laws, regulations, institutions, rules, and ordinances.

4. To settle or fix; to confirm; as, to establish a person, society or corporation, in possessions or privileges.

5. To make firm, to confirm, to ratify what has been previously set or made.

6. To be established is to be recognized.

7. To be established is to be distinguished.

8. To be established is to be distinctly elevated.

9. To be established is someone or something to be accepted in its sphere of influence.

10. To be established is to be declared legitimate and legal.

11. To be established is when you are validated beyond a reasonable doubt.

12. To be established is to be settled securely and unconditionally.

13. To be established is to be markedly superior and

above average.

14. To be established demonstrates the superiority of the Kingdom of God.

15. To be established is to settle or fix what is wavering, doubtful, or weak; to confirm.

16. To establish is to confirm; to fulfill; to make good.

When you *Decree* and *Declare,* it brings the establishment of the matter in the earth realm and your sphere.

"Thou shalt also Decree a thing, and it shall be established unto thee" (Job 22:28).

Why Decree a Thing?

1. Words have the power of life and death.

2. Words are destinations.

3. Words are involved in every new season in your life.

4. Your tongue steers your life.

5. God Works through Your Words.

"I create the fruit of the lips: Peace, peace to him who is far off and to him who is near," says the LORD, "And I will heal him" (Isaiah 57:19).

Note what the Lord is saying in this passage: *"I create the "fruit" of the lips.* What kind of fruit is proceeding from your mouth? Are you giving the Lord words (substance) that He can work with, which is His Word? *"He said His Word would not return void"* *(Isaiah 55:11).*

How does it return to Him? The Word returns to Him **when we speak it. This is a powerful principle.** Immediately, at the beginning of your circumstances or trial, get your faith into motion by declaring who God is and what He has promised to do for you.

"In the beginning was the Word" (*John 1:1*)

Make the Word your **Beginning** in every area in life.

"The mouth of the righteous is a well of life." *(Proverbs 10:11).*

"The mouth of the upright will deliver them" *(Proverbs 12:6).*

"A man will be satisfied with good by the fruit of his mouth" Proverbs 12:14

"The tongue of the wise promotes health" *(Proverbs 12:18).*

"The eyes of the LORD preserve knowledge, but He overthrows the words of the faithless"

(Proverbs 22:12).

"This Book of the Law (The Word) shall not depart from your mouth; but you shall meditate in it day and night, that you may observe to do according to all that is written in it; for then you will make your way prosperous, and then you will have good success" (Joshua 1:8).

"So shall My word be that goes forth from My mouth; It shall not return to Me void, but it shall accomplish what I please, and it shall prosper in the thing for which I sent it."
Isaiah 55:11

God's Word will not fail when it is believed in the heart and spoken forth in faith - The Lord God says so! *It is so and cannot be otherwise!*

"You will also decree a thing, And it will be established for you; So light will shine on your ways" (Job 22:28).

Whatever you Decree trust that it is established.

God gives us the power to declare and decree *"Life and death are in the power of the tongue"* (Proverbs 18:21).

Legislate, confirm, settle, summons, and authorize.

In Peter's epistles, we learn that we are a royal priesthood. It speaks of royalty like a king ruling and reigning.

I DECREE that you are a King and a Priest. Kings make decrees, not pleas. That's why the Bible says,

"Where the word of a king is, there is power,
"Dunamis Power" (Ecclesiastes 8:10)

As a king and priest, your words are backed with divine authority. When you pray, you issue commands as a king and minister to God as a priest. Kings don't beg they rule with Supreme Authority. Therefore, having the awareness and understanding that you're a king and priest unto God will cease all weak prayers from your life. Every word spoken is pregnant with creative power. These decrees give birth to whatever we speak. Whether it be good or bad, life or death, when you speak the Word of God, that Word does not return void.

A closed mouth is a closed destiny. Decree your destiny with Quantum Prayer Leaps! **So, DECREE:**

I am a priest and a king.

I reign in life through Jesus Christ.

I rule over Satan and his house.

I tread on serpents and scorpions. Nothing they try to do

can harm me.

I am under God's protection.

I declare Psalm 91.

I have the keys of the kingdom of God.

What I bind, heaven binds. What I loose, heaven looses.

I bind all forces of evil in my life.

I loose all the blessings of God into my life.

1

LEAP

The word "Leap" means to move quickly or suddenly: It means to jump from one position to another; to move or act quickly; to rise as if with a spring; to pass over. It also means rapid progress, sudden, and exponential increase. It means to make advances and progress with leaps and bounds. To propel oneself quickly upward or a long way; spring or jump: To change rapidly or abruptly from one condition to another.

We are being challenged to leap off the ledge of the past decade and grab onto the trapeze bar of the next decade, which would demonstrate our "trust" in the instructor, rope, apparatus, and promise of the future. Even though this bar seems like a couple of feet from our outstretched arms, in terms of the calendar and timing, standing precariously on this ledge that will launch us into the air, as we Leap, it will seem like its miles away.

Leaping always entertains feelings of fear, doubt,

and indecision that come in not knowing if you would be able to jump far enough if your hands would be able to grab hold of that steel bar if you would have the strength in your arms to keep yourself from falling if the safety rope would be able to catch you should you miss or if the instructor would let go due to negligence or incompetence.

These thoughts and uncertainties are what we face each day in our lives and with our dreams, aspirations, and promises of our future. Sometimes we feel like we're on a reasonably firm "ledge" in life, albeit precarious at times. We have the amazing grace of God, incredible family and friends, and fantastic opportunities. Yet, despite that foundational stability and a history of past "leaps," resulting in fruitful endeavors, we still struggle with letting go and stepping off and leaping into the next that God has for us.

> *"For I know the plans I have for you," declares the Lord, "plans to prosper you and not to harm you, plans to give you hope and a future" (Jeremiah 29:11).*

This verse alone should be enough for any of us to trust our desires and dreams to the Lord. Most of us would whole-heartily acknowledge He has our best interest in mind and knows the plans He has for us. However, when it comes to jumping off of our comfortable ledge or letting go of our (safety) rope, many of us wait until we are assured of the next step and can visibly see (or hold) that next rein before letting go, frequently too late and missing that opportunity.

I DECREE that you will not be too late, nor will you miss your opportunity to quantum leap into what the Lord has for you in this next decade.

Our actions become based more upon calculated, self-determined moves rather than "Faith" in His plan and taking intentional steps towards it. God does give us the desires of our hearts often in a more significant way than we could have ever imagined, but we sometimes delay or derail it if we aren't obedient to the little things along the way.

Often, we don't see how an obstacle, broken relationship, dissatisfying job, inconvenience, or mistake at the time is something that will help us get closer to leaping towards fulfilling our purpose. Instead of sticking with a situation or taking a chance just because we don't see where it's leading, we miss out on an opportunity we were meant to experience, which would have led us to where we were supposed to be.

I DECLARE that in this next decade, you will not miss *your opportunities.*

The original Greek word for leap is **Skirtao:**

1. To Leap.
2. Akin to skairo (meaning to skip); or to jump, i.e., Sympathetically move (as the quickening of a fetus).
3. to Skip, to Jump, to Vault and to Kick. (skeer-tah'-o)

Leap means to JUMP

1. The act of leaping or jumping. To propel oneself upward or over a distance in single quick motion or series of such movements, **defying the law of gravity**. Defying the power of everything that has held you down and hindered you from attaining the heights of purpose and destiny ordained for you. Jump - **A sudden and decisive increase;** "a jump in attendance," a leap increase; change resulting in an increase; as in "the increase is scheduled for next month."

Quantum Leap

1. A sudden, highly significant advance, breakthrough sudden substantial increase or

advance; "this may not ensure success, but it will represent a quantum leap from where you were. Jump; rise in rank and status.

Leap means to SKIP

1. The distance traversed by a leap or skip. A significant move forward; to skip means to or pass over; bypass to elevate, esp. in rank, by causing to skip or pass rapidly through intermediate stages.

2. A leaping or jumping movement, especially a gait in which hops and steps alternate.

3. An act of passing over something; an omission.

4. To pass from point to point, omitting or disregarding what intervenes:

5. To be promoted in and beyond the next regular class, grade, or step in the process of qualifying you.

6. To be advanced two or more classes or grades at once.

Leap means to VAULT

1. To spring clear of the ground, with the feet; to jump; to vault; as, a man leaps over a fence, to cause to leap over an obstacle: **vault** - the act of

jumping over an obstacle, hurdle the act of jumping; propelling yourself off the ground

2. To pass over by a leap or jump; as, to leap over a wall, to leap, as to or from a position or over something: *to vault over the net.*

Leap means to KICK

1. Means to spring or move suddenly, as by extending the leg away from the body; and striking out with the foot or feet.

2. To bound; to move swiftly by giving a vigorous blow with the foot.

Leap Means;

1. To move with bounds: to spring upward or forward: to jump: to rush with vehemence.

2. To bound over: to cause to leap:

2020 is a Leap Year, the 1st year of the next Decade.

A Leap' Year is every fourth year—of 365 days, adding one day in February, making it 366 days — 2020 take a **Leap in the dark,** an act of which we cannot foresee the consequences.

Take the Leap of Faith into Destiny by releasing declarations of faith through prayer.

Leap Means;

3. A **sudden and decisive increase** as in *"a jump in attendance."*

4. **A change resulting in an increase**, as in "the increase is scheduled for next month."

I DECREE you will leap into a season of decisive increase, in Jesus' name.

I DECREE you will Quantum Leap into dimensions of change resulting in an exponential increase, in Jesus' name!

Quantum Leap Means;

5. A sudden, **highly significant advance, breakthrough** sudden massive increase or advance; "this may not ensure success, but it will represent a quantum leap from where you were. Jump; rise in rank and status.

I DECREE, you will experience a sudden and decisive increase, quantum leaps, and a rise in rank and status in every area of your life, financially, spiritually, minister ally, and relationally, in Jesus' name!

Leap Means;

5. To move forward by leaps and bounds.

I DECREE Your life will move forward by leaps and

bounds through the path of destiny in this next Decade, in Jesus' name!

Leap Means;

6. To pass abruptly from one Status to another as in *"leap into fame."*

I DECREE You will pass abruptly from one status of living to another. From Poverty to Prosperity, from Lack to Abundance, from Beneath to Above, from Sickness to Health, from Lack to Plenty, in Jesus' name!

Every **"TINY"** leap in the big picture of life doesn't seem like much, however, many of these jumps, in the course of a lifetime, add up to a life lived to the fullest taking advantage of every break, not allowing obstacles or others to deter you from where you could be.

Everyone has their destiny; not everyone chooses to follow it. Leapers are faith led and trust God completely based on His word. Trusting God in "thy" will also means trusting His path to get us there and letting go of ours.

Have you ever stopped to wonder why it is that every four years, February has an extra day?

A leap year, or intercalary year, is where the calendar contains one additional day to keep them in line with the seasons. Over time, rigid calendars cause each year to drift and fall out of alignment with the seasons. To counter this, inserting (or intercalating) an extra day into the year stops the drift from happening. A year that is not a leap year is called a common year hence making a Leap year an "Un-Common Year."

I DECREE that as you enter into this next year and decade, you will experience Un-usual and Un-common manifestations and fulfillment of God's promises to you."

PRAYER DECLARATIONS

As I Quantum Prayer Leap into the Next Decade:

I DECLARE that I will quantum Leap and experience un-common grace.

I DECLARE that I will quantum Leap and experience un-common favor.

I DECLARE that I will quantum Leap and experience un-common healings.

I DECLARE that I will quantum Leap and experience un-common increase.

I DECLARE that I will quantum Leap and experience un-common abundance.

I DECLARE that I will quantum Leap and experience un-common opportunities.

I DECLARE that I will quantum Leap and experience un-common open doors.

I DECLARE that I will quantum Leap and experience un-common strength.

I DECLARE that I will quantum Leap and experience *un-common joy.*

I DECLARE that I will quantum Leap and experience un-common supplies of the Anointing, in Jesus' Name!

How do we get leap years? The name "leap year" probably comes from the fact that while a fixed date in the Gregorian calendar advances typically one day of the week from one year to the next, the day of the week in the 12 months following the leap day (from March 1 through February 28 of the following year) will advance two days due to the extra day (thus "leaping over" one of the days in the week). For example, Christmas Day (December 25) fell on a Tuesday in 2012, Wednesday in 2013, Thursday in 2014, and Friday in 2015 but then **"Leapt"** over Saturday to fall on a Sunday in 2016, which means Double.

The spiritual meaning is that this becomes **YOUR YEAR OF DOUBLE**.

I DECREE that as you enter into this next year and

decade, you will Quantum Leap and experience unusual and uncommon manifestations of DOUBLE.

This is a promise of God to restore His people to the original position. In effect, after the order of Jonah, anything that has swallowed you, your destiny, your family, your dreams will vomit you out, and you will gain lost ground, in Jesus' name!

God knows your pains, the things you have lost in your life, your lost relationships, dreams, past mistakes, lost investments, failed issues, and projects. However, there is an account of how God will restore to you in such mighty abundance in

> *"Which says, "Instead of your former shame you will have a **double portion**; and instead of humiliation your people will shout for joy over their portion. Therefore in their land they will possess **double** [what they had forfeited]; Everlasting joy will be theirs" (Isaiah 61:7 [AMP]).*

PRAYER DECLARATIONS

As I Quantum Prayer Leap into the Next Decade:

I DECREE that I will quantum Leap and experience Double in every area of your life.

I DECREE that instead of my Shame, I will quantum Leap, and I will have and experience Double Honor.

> *"For your shame ye shall have **Double Honor**; and for confusion they shall rejoice in their portion: therefore in their land they shall possess **the double:** everlasting joy shall be unto them" (Isaiah 61:7).*

I DECREE that my land, territory, business, and ministry shall possess **"the Double"** and everlasting joy shall be my potion.

> *"Turn you to the stronghold, ye prisoners of hope: even today do I declare that I will **Restore Double** unto thee" (Zechariah 9:12).*

I DECREE Double Restoration in every area.

PRAYER DECLARATIONS

I DECREE I will quantum Leap into the Double restoration of un-common favor.

I DECREE I will quantum Leap into the Double restoration of un-common increase.

I DECREE I will quantum Leap into the Double restoration of health.

I DECREE I will quantum Leap into the Double

restoration of wealth.

I DECREE I will quantum Leap into the Double restoration of authority.

I DECREE I will quantum Leap into the Restoration of **Double Pay:**

> *"If a man shall deliver unto his neighbor money or stuff to keep, and it be stolen out of the man's house; if the thief be found, let him **pay double**"* (*Exodus 22:7*).

PRAYER DECLARATIONS

I DECREE I will quantum Leap into Double Pay for all your Labor.

I DECREE I will quantum Leap into Double Pay for all your inputs and contributions.

I DECREE I will quantum Leap into Double Pay for all your hours of hard work.

I DECREE I will quantum Leap into Double Pay for all your future Labor.

I DECREE I will quantum Leap into Double Pay for all the works of your hands in the next decade, in Jesus' name!

I DECREE the Restoration of Double Honor.

*"Let the elders that rule well be counted worthy of **Double Honor** especially they who labor in the word and doctrine"*
(1Timothy 5:17).

PRAYER DECLARATIONS

I DECREE 2020, and the next decade you will receive Double Honor for all my hard work.

I DECREE 2020, and the next decade I will quantum Leap into my business, and I will receive Double Honor and recognition.

I DECREE 2020, and the next decade I will quantum Leap into ministry, and I will receive Double Honor and recognition, in Jesus' name!

I DECLARE the Restoration of Lost Years.

"And I will restore to you the years that the locust hath eaten, the cankerworm, and the caterpillar, and the palmerworm, my great army which I sent among you" (Joel 2:25).

I DECREE the Restoration of Lost Years of business.

I DECREE the Restoration of Lost Years of ministry.

I DECREE the Restoration of Lost Years of health.

I DECREE the Restoration of Lost Years of elevation

and promotion.

I DECREE the Restoration of Lost Years of advancement and enlargement, in Jesus' name!

Our God is a Restorer; He is ready to restore all your wasted years and put an end to all chronic delays. God knows your need; He is willing to compensate you and give you double for your trouble.

Don't just expect one thing, because God can give you not just double for your trouble but can give you triple or multiple to compensate you for time lost, and He will wipe away your years of sorrow, toiling and waiting.

I DECREE Double Destruction Against All Enemies.

*"Let them be confounded that persecute me, but let not me be confounded: let them be dismayed, but let not me be dismayed: bring upon them the day of evil, and **destroy them with double destruction"** (*Jeremiah 17:18).

PRAYER DECLARATIONS

I DECREE Double Destruction Against All Enemies of my destiny.

I DECREE Double Destruction Against All Enemies of my purpose.

I DECREE Double Destruction Against All Enemies of my health.

I DECREE Double Destruction Against All Enemies of my progress.

I DECREE Double Destruction Against All Enemies of my advancement.

I DECREE Double Destruction Against All Enemies of my elevation.

I DECREE Double Destruction Against All Enemies of my enlargement.

I DECREE Double Destruction Against All demonic and satanic entities that orchestrate my demise.

I DECREE Double Destruction Against All demonic projections and determination, in Jesus' name!

I DECREE The Sword Will Do Double Damage Against All Enemies.

> *"You therefore, son of man, prophesy, And strike your hands together. The third time **let the sword do Double Damage.** It is the sword that slays, the sword that slays the great men, that enters their private chambers" (Ezekiel 21:14,* NKJV).

PRAYER DECLARATIONS

I DECREE the Sword of The Spirit will do Double Destruction Against All Enemies of health, wealth, wellbeing, and family.

I DECREE the Sword of The Spirit will do Double Destruction Against All demonic and satanic entities that *orchestrate my demise.*

I DECREE the Sword of The Spirit will do Double Destruction Against All generational and ancestral powers that threaten my future.

I DECREE the Sword of The Spirit will do Double Destruction Against All destructive mindsets and belief systems that threaten my future, in Jesus' name!

2020 is a Leap Year. Leap years occur in four-year cycles. It is called a leap year because, in the month of February, the shortest month, an additional day is added. A usual year has 365 days, so in a leap year, there are 366 days making it a year with an added day.

I DECREE that as you enter into this next year and decade, you will experience unusual and uncommon **Divine Additions** in every area of your life.

"And God remembered Rachel, and God hearkened to her, and opened her womb. And

*she conceived, and bare a son; and said, God hath taken away my reproach: And she called his name Joseph; and said, The LORD shall **Add** to me another son" (Genesis 30:22-24).*

PRAYER DECLARATIONS

I DECREE I will quantum Leap into divine Additions of un-common favor.

I DECREE I will quantum Leap into divine Additions of un-common increase.

I DECREE I will quantum Leap into divine Additions of un-common resources.

I DECREE I will quantum Leap into divine Additions of un-common Life Spans.

> *"Go, and say to Hezekiah, Thus saith the LORD, the God of David thy father, I have heard thy prayer, I have seen thy tears: behold, **I will Add** unto thy days fifteen years" (Isaiah 38:5).*

I DECREE I will quantum Leap into divine Additions of un-common faith, virtue, and knowledge.

I DECREE I will quantum Leap into divine Additions daily to the church, in Jesus' name!

2

LEAP OVER WALLS

*"For by You I can run against a troop; by my
God **I can leap over a wall**" (*2 Samuel 22:30).

In the Old, Testament walls were used to provide
security, protection, shelter, and belonging.

*"Therefore he said unto Judah, Let us build
these cities, and make about them walls, and
towers, gates, and bars, while the land is yet
before us; because we have sought the LORD
our God, we have sought him, and he hath given
us rest on every side. So they built and
prospered" (2 Chronicles 14:7).*

*"He that hath no rule over his own spirit is like
a city that is broken down, and without walls"
(Proverbs 25:28)*

But walls also were used to imprison, confine, limit,
divide and stand as an impediment or hindrance to one's

access to territory, or ground ordained for them.

"Joseph is a fruitful bough, even a fruitful bough by a well; whose branches run over the wall." (Genesis 49:22).

[**Joseph's Vine bounded over the walls of imprisonment and confinement**] that tried to impede him from fulfilling his Destiny as Prime Minister of Egypt and as the savior of his people.

*NOW JERICHO [**a fenced town with high walls**] was tightly closed because of the Israelites; no one went out or came in. Joshua 6:1 AMP*

There are geographical regions, territories, towns, cities, and nations assigned to you as part of your Destiny inheritance. Still, the enemy has spiritually fenced them and put up invisible walls and barriers to stop and impede you. They represent the spirit that stands in one's way to restrict them from performing in their full potential. It restricts one to function far below what heaven has ordained hence hindering their progress, level of achievement, and success.

In this Decade of Destiny, you will overcome them and Leap over geographical walls, regional walls, territorial walls in towns, cities, and nations assigned to you as part of your Destiny inheritance, but the enemy has spiritually fenced them and put up invisible walls and barriers to stop and impede you, in Jesus' name!

Walls also are when one is limited in every sphere of life – academically, martially, socially, politically, spiritually, financially, and even in business. To suffer limitation in life is to have one's level of joy, success, and achievement determined by other people, especially one's enemies. A barrier is placed in such people's way to greatness. They may have the potentials for greatness, excellence, and prosperity, but there is an extent to which they are allowed to go in life.

David knew what he was talking about when he said that he could run against a troop and leap over a wall. He lived it out! The Bible tells us that he spoke the words of this song to the Lord after He had delivered him from all his enemies (Plural).

The walls David had to leap over were literal. Today walls are not only literal or physical but spiritual, mental, and emotional. However, know that whatever your walls are your life, that you by the strength of God, you will Quantum Leap over them through these Prayer Decrees and Declarations:

PRAYER DECLARATIONS

I DECREE that in this next year and decade, I will Quantum Leap over walls of discouragement and despair.

I DECREE that in this next year and decade, I will Quantum leap over the walls of doubt and unbelief.

I DECREE that in this next year and decade, I will Quantum Leap over the walls of resentment, bitterness, and anger.

I DECREE that in this next year and decade, I will Quantum Leap over the walls of loneliness and isolation.

I DECREE that in this next year and decade, I will Quantum Leap over the walls of infirmity, sickness, and disease.

I DECREE that in this next year and decade, I will Quantum Leap over the walls of depression, oppression, and suppression.

I DECREE that in this next year and decade, I will Quantum Leap over the walls of fear and timidity.

I DECREE that in this next year and decade, I will Quantum Leap over the walls of anxiety and conflicting emotions.

I DECREE that in this next year and decade, I will Quantum Leap over the walls of helplessness hopelessness.

I DECREE that in this next year and decade, I will Quantum Leap over the walls of fatigue, exhaustion, tiredness, and fatigue.

I DECREE that in this next year and decade, I will Quantum Leap over the walls of dread, mental distress, emotional distress, psychological distress, physical distress, and financial distress.

I DECREE that in this next year and decade, I will Quantum Leap over the walls of limitations and restrictions.

Limitations can be found in any aspect of our lives; marriage, finances, spiritual walk, education, relationship, health, job, and ministry, just to mention a few.

I DECREE that in this next year and decade, I will Quantum Leap over the walls of opposition and resistance.

Whatever wall you are facing, I declare with you, that you can and will Quantum Leap over it! And you are going to leap over it, in Jesus' Mighty Name!

3

LEAP FOR JOY

*"Rejoice and be glad at such a time and exult and **leap for joy,** for behold, your reward is rich and great and strong and intense and abundant in heaven; for even so their forefathers treated the prophets" (Luke 6:23, AMP).*

One of the initial manifestations and gifts of salvation is **JOY**.

"Restore unto me the Joy of thy salvation; and uphold me with thy free spirit" (Psalm 51:12).

JOY is expressed when God defends His people.

"But let all those that put their trust in thee rejoice: let them ever shout for Joy, because thou defendest them: let them also that love thy name be joyful in thee" (Psalm 5:11).

JOY is expressed when in the Presence of God.

"Thou wilt shew me the path of life: in thy

presence is fulness of Joy; at thy right hand there are pleasures forevermore"
(Psalm 16:11).

JOY is expressed when your dark and weeping night season ends, and it's the dawning of a new day.

"For his anger endureth but a moment; in his favour is life: weeping may endure for a night, but joy cometh in the morning" (Psalm 30:5).

JOY is expressed when you see the harvest of seeds sown.

"Turn again our captivity, O LORD, as the streams in the south. They that sow in tears shall reap in Joy" (Psalm 126:4-5).

JOY is expressed when you see the redeemed returning, and when they obtain gladness and joy become theirs and no more sorrow and mourning.

"Therefore the redeemed of the LORD shall return, and come with singing unto Zion; and everlasting Joy shall be upon their head: they shall obtain gladness and joy; and sorrow and mourning shall flee away" (Isaiah 51:11).

JOY is expressed when Jesus promises to fill you with His **JOY** until it overflows.

*"I have told you these things, that My Joy and delight may be in you, and that your **Joy and gladness may be of Full measure and complete and overflowing.**" John 15:11 AMP*

I DECREE that in the Decade of Destiny, you will QUANTUM LEAP with overflowing **JOY**.

"Rejoice and be glad at such a time and exult and leap for Joy, for behold, your reward is rich and great and strong and intense and abundant in heaven; for even so their forefathers treated the prophets" (Luke 6:23, AMP).

PRAYER DECLARATIONS

I DECREE that in this next year and decade, I will Rejoice and be glad at this time and exult and Quantum Leap for **JOY** because my reward is rich and great and strong and intense and abundant in heaven.

I DECREE that in this next year and decade, I will Quantum Leap as God Restores unto me the **JOY** of His salvation; and uphold me with His free spirit.

I DECREE that in this next year and decade, I will Quantum Leap with **JOY** unspeakable full of glory.

I DECREE that in this next year and decade, I will Quantum Leap with **JOY** when the Lord turns again my captivity, and when I reap what I've sown in tears.

I DECREE that in this next year and decade, I will Quantum Leap with **JOY** for my weeping has ended. It's my season of Joy Cometh in every area of my life."

I will Quantum Leap, for **JOY** Cometh to my home.

I will Quantum Leap, for **JOY** Cometh to my family.

I will Quantum Leap, for **JOY** Cometh to my ministry.

I will Quantum Leap, for **JOY** Cometh to my business.

I will Quantum Leap, for **JOY** Cometh life.

I DECREE that in this next year and decade, I will Quantum Leap with **JOY** for behold, my reward is rich and great and strong and intense and abundant.

4

LEAP FORTH; LEAP AND PRAISE GOD

*"And **leaping forth** he stood and began to walk,*
and he went into the temple with them, walking
*and **leaping** and praising God" (Acts 3:8).*

The scripture, as mentioned above, was the account of the man who had been lame from his mother's womb until a Quantum Leap Prayer command was made by Apostle Peter. The word "Leaping" occurs twice in one verse. Remember, the word "Leap" means to jump from one position to another; to move or act quickly; to rise above the pull of gravity; to spring. It also means moving forward or making progress in leaps and bounds.

"Strengthen ye the weak hands, and confirm the
feeble knees. Say to them that are of a fearful
heart, Be strong, fear not: behold, your God will
come with vengeance, even God with a
recompense; He will come and save you. Then
the eyes of the blind shall be opened, and the
*ears of the deaf shall be unstopped. **Then shall***

the Lame man Leap as an hart, and the tongue of the dumb sing: for in the wilderness shall waters break out, and streams in the desert" (Isaiah 35:3-6).

PRAYER DECLARATIONS

I DECREE that in this next year and decade, I will Quantum Leap forth, stand up, walk and enter into my Destiny, and praise the Lord.

I DECREE that in this next year and decade, I will Quantum Leap forth, stand up, walk and enter into my opportunities and praise the Lord.

I DECREE that in this next year and decade, I will Quantum Leap and declare Then shall my Lame marriage Leap as a hart.

I DECREE that in this next year and decade, I will Quantum Leap and declare Then shall my Lame finances Leap as a hart.

I DECREE that in this next year and decade, I will Quantum Leap and declare Then shall my Lame ministry Leap as a hart.

I DECREE that in this next year and decade, I will Quantum Leap and declare Then shall my Lame business Leap as a hart.

I DECREE that in this next year and decade, I will Quantum Leap and declare Then shall my Lame zeal and passion Leap as a hart.

I DECREE that in this next year and decade, I will Quantum Leap, make rapid progress, sudden, and decisive increase, and exponential turnaround praising the Lord, in Jesus' name.

5

LEAP IN THE WOMB OF DESTINY

*"And it happened, when Elizabeth heard the greeting of Mary, that the babe **leaped in her womb;** and Elizabeth was filled with the Holy Spirit" (Luke 1:41).*

*"For indeed, as soon as **the voice** of your greeting **sounded** in my ears, **the babe leaped in my womb** for joy" (Luke 1:44).*

Destinies are carried in wombs.

*"Before I formed you in the **Womb** I knew [and] approved of you [as My chosen instrument], and before you were born I separated and set you apart, consecrating you; [and] I appointed you as a prophet to the nations" (Jeremiah 1:5).*

*"Listen, O isles, unto me; and hearken, ye people, from far; The LORD hath called me from the **Womb**; from the bowels of my mother hath he made mention of my name" (Isaiah*

49:1).

*"But thou art He that took me out of the **Womb**: thou didst make me hope when I was upon my mother's breasts. I was cast upon thee from the **Womb**: thou art my God from my mother's belly" (Psalm 22:9- 10).*

The Womb is the uterus or matrix of a female; that part where the young embryo is conceived and nourished till its birth. But the womb has deep spiritual connotations. Destiny wombs are always targeted wombs. A womb of Destiny can be miscarried, aborted, vandalized, sabotaged, undermined, or rendered barren.

Some of you like Elizabeth though you have conceived and are carrying your destiny, vision, or dream, yet there no sign of life. Everything in this Decade of Destiny will be contingent on Voice and Sound to activate what you are carrying.

There are scriptures that enemies can twist and use to pray against Destiny Wombs, e.g.:

*"Give them, O LORD: what wilt thou give? give them a miscarrying **womb** and dry breasts."*
Hosea 9:14

I DECREE that in the Decade of Destiny, you will

QUANTUM LEAP, and your Womb of Destiny will never miscarry, nor will your spiritual breasts dry up.

Your destinies can also be empowered for fulfillment from the womb.

> "*And Mary arose in those days, and went into the hill country with haste, into a city of Judah; And entered into the house of Zacharias, and saluted Elisabeth. **And it came to pass, that, when Elisabeth heard the salutation of Mary, the babe Leaped in her womb; and Elisabeth was filled with the Holy Ghost:** And she spake out with a loud voice, and said, Blessed art thou among women, and blessed is the fruit of thy womb. And whence is this to me, that the mother of my Lord should come to me? **For, lo, as soon as the voice of thy salutation sounded in mine ears, the babe Leaped in my womb for joy.** And blessed is she that believed: for there shall be a performance of those things which were told her from the Lord.*" Luke 1:39-45

When your Womb of Destiny is empowered by the Holy Spirit, what you are carrying Leaps for Joy because He is the Spirit of Joy.

PRAYER DECLARATIONS

I DECREE that in this next year and decade, my Destiny in the womb will Quantum Leap, Jump, Skip, and Kick for Joy.

I DECREE that in this next year and decade, my Vision in the womb will Quantum Leap, Jump, Skip, and Kick for Joy.

I DECREE that in this next year and decade, my Purpose in the womb will Quantum Leap, Jump, Skip, and Kick for Joy.

I DECREE that in this next year and decade, my Seeds in the womb will Quantum Leap, Jump, Skip, and Kick for Joy.

I DECREE that in this next year and decade, my Dreams in the womb will Quantum Leap, Jump, Skip, and Kick for Joy.

I DECREE that in this next year and decade, my Plans in the womb will Quantum Leap, Jump, Skip, and Kick for Joy.

I DECREE that in this next year and decade, my Womb will never become a Tomb.

I DECREE that in this next year and decade, my Womb

will never miscarry my Destiny.

I DECREE that in this next year and decade, my Womb will never be paralyzed.

I DECREE that in this next year and decade, my Womb is covered and sealed by the blood of Jesus.

6

LEAP INTO LOVE

*[The Beloved's Request] [The Shulamite] "The voice of my beloved! Behold, he comes **Leaping** upon the mountains, Skipping upon the hills." Song of Solomon 2:8*

*"I opened for my beloved, But my beloved had turned away and was gone. **My heart leaped up when he spoke.** I sought him, but I could not find him; I called him, but he gave me no answer." Song of Solomon 5:6*

I DECREE that in the Decade of Destiny, your Beloved will QUANTUM LEAP; he/she will come skipping upon the hills looking for you.

I DECREE that in the Decade of Destiny you will open for your Beloved and he/she will QUANTUM LEAP; he/she will Not turn away, your heart will Leap with up when he speaks, and when you call he/she will answer.

PRAYER DECLARATIONS

I DECREE that in this next year and decade, I will Quantum Leap, Jump, Skip, and Kick for into true love.

I DECREE that in this next year and decade, I will Quantum Leap, Jump, Skip, and Kick into love that endures long.

I DECREE that in this next year and decade, I will Quantum Leap, Jump, Skip, and Kick into love that is patient and kind.

I DECREE that in this next year and decade, I will Quantum Leap, Jump, Skip, and Kick into love that never is envious nor boils over with jealousy.

I DECREE that in this next year and decade, I will Quantum Leap, Jump, Skip, and Kick into love that is not boastful or vainglorious.

I DECREE that in this next year and decade, I will Quantum Leap, Jump, Skip, and Kick into love that does not display itself haughtily.

I DECREE that in this next year and decade, I will Quantum Leap, Jump, Skip, and Kick into love that is not conceited (arrogant and inflated with pride).

I DECREE that in this next year and decade, I will

Quantum Leap, Jump, Skip, and Kick into love that is not rude (unmannerly) and does not act unbecomingly.

I DECREE that in this next year and decade, I will Quantum Leap, Jump, Skip, and Kick into love that does not insist on its own rights or its own way, for it is not self-seeking.

I DECREE that in this next year and decade, I will Quantum Leap, Jump, Skip, and Kick into love that is not touchy or fretful or resentful.

I DECREE that in this next year and decade, I will Quantum Leap, Jump, Skip, and Kick into love that takes no account of the evil done to it [it pays no attention to a suffered wrong].

I DECREE that in this next year and decade, I will Quantum Leap, Jump, Skip, and Kick into love that does not rejoice at injustice and unrighteousness but rejoices when right and truth prevail.

I DECREE that in this next year and decade, I will Quantum Leap, Jump, Skip, and Kick into love that bears up under anything and everything that comes, love that is ever ready to believe the best of every person, love, whose hopes are fadeless under all circumstances, and endures everything [without weakening].

I DECREE that in this next year and decade, I will Quantum Leap, Jump, Skip, and Kick into love that never fails [never fades out or becomes obsolete or comes to an end].

7

DAILY DECLARATIONS

You have the authority to decree a thing.

*"Thou shalt also **Decree** a thing, and it shall be established unto thee: and the light shall shine upon thy ways" (Job 22:28).*

Speak these declarations over your life DAILY with expectation:

I DECREE the keys of the kingdom of heaven have been given to me, and whatsoever I bind on earth is bound in heaven, and whatsoever I loose on earth is loosed in heaven (Matthew 16:19).

I DECREE no weapon formed against me shall prosper, and every tongue that shall rise against me in judgment shall be condemned (Isaiah 54:17).

I DECREE I am blessed coming in and blessed going out. I am the head and not the tail, above only, and not beneath (Deuteronomy 28:13).

I DECREE I am strong in the Lord and the power of His might as I put on the whole armor of God and stand against all the wiles of the devil (Ephesians 6:11).

I DECREE my steps are ordered every day by the Lord (Psalm 37:23).

I DECREE all things work together for my good because I love God and are called according to His purpose (Romans 8:28).

I DECREE God is my refuge and strength, a very present help in times of trouble (Psalms 46:1).

I DECREE God has not given me the spirit of fear, but of power, love, and a sound mind (2 Timothy 1:7).

I DECREE the LORD renews my strength; I mount up with wings as eagles; I run, and shall not be weary, walk, and faint not (Isaiah 40:31).

I DECREE the favor of God. If God be for me, who can be against me? (Romans 8:31).

I DECREE I give, and it shall be given back to me; good measure, pressed down, shaken together, and running over, shall men give into my bosom (Luke 6:38).

I DECREE I delight myself in the LORD, and he gives me the desires of my heart (Psalms 37:4).

I DECREE I have the peace of God that passes all understanding (Philippians 4:7).

I DECREE I am a believer with signs follow me. In the Name of Jesus, I cast out devils, speak with new tongues, take up serpents, and if I drink any deadly thing, it will not harm me; I lay hands on the sick, and they recover (Mark 16:17-19).

I DECREE greater is He that lives in me than he that lives in the world (1 John 4:4).

I DECREE My God supplies all of my needs according to His riches in glory by Christ Jesus (Philippians 4:19).

I DECREE by His stripes; I am healed (1 Peter 2:24).

I DECREE I am born of God, and the evil one cannot touch me (1 John 5:18).

I DECREE I call on the Lord, and He answers me and shows me great and mighty things I know not of (Jeremiah 33:3).

I DECREE I have been given the power to tread on serpents and scorpions, and overall the power of the enemy: and nothing shall by any means hurt me. (Luke 10:19)

I DECREE God gives me the treasures of darkness and

hidden riches of secret places that I may know that the LORD is God. (Isaiah 45:3)

I DECREE God is not a man that he should lie to me, neither the son of man that he should change His mind. The things he has said, he will do, and the things he has spoken he will make good. (Numbers 23:19)

I DECREE wealth and riches shall be in my house because I fear the Lord. (Psalm 112:3)

I DECREE the kingdom of God come, in my life, family, marriage, ministry, relationships, and work. (Matthew 6:10)

I DECREE I am satisfied with the words of my mouth because life and death are in the power of my tongue. Proverbs 18:20

I DECREE, with absolute faith by God's eternal Spirit of grace and mercy that I now inhabit heavenly places and sit high above all principality and power, might and dominions and every name that is named! Thus, I work, walk, talk, and think in authority and exercise my right to be rich and live the abundant lifestyle given unto me by Christ Jesus, in Jesus' name (Ephesians 1:12-23, 2:4).

I DECREE with absolute faith that today going forward. I operate outside this world's system and accumulate wealth, health, riches, honor, and blessing supernaturally by divine providence, favor, mercy, in Jesus' name! (Philippians 4:19).

I DECREE with absolute faith that as an heir of God and joint-heir with Christ I have a right to be rich, prosperous and well satisfied in all areas of my life with plenty to give and enough to meet all needs that arise with plenty to spare, in Jesus' name (2 Corinthians 9:6-12)

I DECREE with absolute faith that the divine will of God is for me to dwell in my wealthy place! Multiple channels of prosperity, riches, health, wealth, abundance, and financial increase come into, invade and saturate my life now in Jesus' name! Deuteronomy 28:1-14

I DECREE with absolute faith that my hearing is acute, fine-tuned, bent toward His heart and magnetized to the voice of the Holy Spirit who shall speak to me, lead and guide me into my wealthy place. Thus, I will trust, follow, and execute the plans of the Spirit to achieve my destination and inhabit this fabulous place (Isaiah 48:15-18).

I DECREE with absolute faith that I have arrived in my wealthy place of abundance, prosperity, riches, spiritual power, wisdom, and blessing!

The blessing of Abraham has exploded in my life, and I now have become a channel for God's unlimited flow of supplies and a vessel prepared for His use, n Jesus' name (Psalm 66:12, 2 Peter 1:3-11, Galatians 3:13-14).

I DECREE with absolute faith that God is my source using many channels, of which I am one, to bless His people and accomplish His will in the earth realm.

As a channel, I open myself up to receive and release by faith, healing, empowerment, salvation, wisdom, knowledge, creative ideas, increase, blessing, the anointing, discernment, love, reconciliation, restoration, deliverance, stability, and grace all, in Jesus' name (Isaiah 60).

I DECREE with absolute faith that I let the wisdom of God overshadow my spirit, mind, soul, and body that I may be guided in what to say, how to say it and to whom to say it to, in Jesus' name (Isaiah 55:11-13).

I DECREE with absolute faith that every day I expect, experience, and manifest the miracles of the kingdom, which validate, vindicate, and confirm the Word of God in the earth realm (Psalm 62:5).

I DECREE with absolute faith that I walk, operate, pray, and speak through the Spirit. I see, hear, and manifest the

74

things of the Spirit through the fruit and gifts of the Spirit of God. Through my spiritual connection with the *righteousness, judgment, and Kingdom* of God, I receive, I am entitled to, and embrace the prepared blessings that have been reserved, revealed, transferred and released into my life, family, and church (1 Corinthians 2:9-12).

I DECREE with absolute faith that today forward, I believe all things are possible through the anointing, the Word, and recognizing God as my source (Luke 1:37).

I DECREE with absolute faith that today, my heart is filled with the presence of God and will forever provide a place for His habitation, demonstration, and power! (2 Corinthians 4:7).

I DECREE with absolute faith that I walk under the anointing of Christ, which has destroyed all yokes, links, chains, and strongholds connected to my life and all those I connect with. Setting all completely, free financially, physically, spiritually, and emotionally (Isaiah 10:27, Jonah 8:32,36, 2 Corinthians 10:3-6).

I DECREE with absolute faith that today I flow in the anointing of Christ, the grace of God, and empowerment of the Holy Spirit for the fulfillment of His will for my life and advancement of humanity, family, and the kingdom. (Isaiah 11:1-4, Luke 10:19-20, Acts 1:8).

I DECREE with absolute faith that the spirit of fear, doubt, unbelief, disobedience, and deception are broken and eliminated from my life, family, ministry, and church. Thus, I now flow with the Trinity in peace, power, wisdom, understanding, knowledge, gifts, skills, talents of the Kingdom of God for the manifestation of His Glory in the earth realm (John 7:38-39, 16:13-16).

I DECREE with absolute faith that from this day forward, I'll never be broke again another day of my life. The anointing has destroyed all yokes, chains, hindrances, restrictions, obstacles, and dams that have blocked all forms of increase, prosperity, advancement, elevations, and promotions that were ordained for the fulfillment of God's will in my life, family, and church (Isaiah 10:27, 2 Corinthians 8:9).

I DECREE with absolute faith that the Lord is my shepherd and I shall not want! He restores my soul, anoints my head, mind, and spirit and makes my soul over ow with joy, peace, power, the anointing, love, vision, dreams, directions, favor, and patience (Psalm 23).

I DECREE with absolute faith that I through, the anointing of God shall not want, have, lack, experience poverty or suffer need but shall be completely supplied with all blessings both natural and spiritual to fulfill my destiny! Thus I attract abundance in all forms, experience financial freedom, become a lender, the head above only, and obtain all resources from God my only source, in the form of gifts, donations, rewards, grants, business transactions, miracles, divine manifestations, wealth transfers and the like that I may excel, advance the Kingdom of God and establish His covenant in the earth realm and bring Glory to His name (1 Chronicles 29:11-12, Deuteronomy 28:1-14).

I DECREE with absolute faith that today, supernatural debt cancellation has taken place in my life, ministry, family and church, wealth, riches, prosperity, all currencies, and financial elevation comes into my life now without delay, in Jesus' name (Genesis 12:1-3, 13:1-2).

I DECREE with absolute faith that today, this is my DECADE of DESTINY DELIVERY AND DESTINY FULFILLMENT, IN JESUS' NAME! AMEN!

.

YOUR COVENANT COMMITMENT TO THE MINISTRY

1. PRAY daily for at least 15 minutes.
2. PRAY daily for divine protection for my family and me, as well as for our worldwide ministry team and their families, and our entire ministry.
3. PRAY daily for a harvest of souls around the world.
4. PRAY daily for your nation, its government, your church leaders, and for spiritual revival.
5. PRAY daily for the urgent prayer requests that come to the ministry from God's people around the globe.
6. PRAY daily for the other prayer warriors in this mighty army.
7. PRAISE God daily for the victories He is pouring upon the lives of His people.

OUR COVENANT COMMITMENT TO YOU

1. My team and I promise to pray daily for you and your loved ones.
2. You will be able to submit your prayer requests and praise reports directly to my private e-mail address explicitly reserved for members of the Prayer Academy, Elite Warriors.
3. We will stand in the gap on your behalf until you get the victory.
4. We will send you e-mails for special events that are occurring, as well as urgent prayer requests from people around the globe.

PRAYER DECLARATION SERIES BY SARAH MORGAN

1. Activating and Affirming God's Prophecies and Promises
2. Affirmations of Faith
3. Blessed State of the Righteous
4. Breaking the Anti-Marriage Spirit
5. Breaking Dream Killers
6. Chain Breakers
7. Children's Prayers
8. Cleansing from Defilement
9. Destroying the Spirit of Stagnancy
10. Finances-Prosperity
11. Healing Prayer
12. Healing is for You
13. I Am Declarations
14. Praying by the Blood of Jesus
15. Prayers for Healing
16. Prayer for Husbands
17. Prophetic Call
18. Pursue and Overtake and Recover
19. Seven Mountain Prayer
20. Supernatural God
21. The Snare is Broken
22. Waiting on the Faithfulness and Loving Kindness of God
23. Weapons of Mass Destruction I
24. Weapons of Mass Destruction II
25. Wisdom
26. Eliezer Lord My Helper
27. When You Pray Not If
28. Quantum Prayer Leap Decrees

ADDITIONAL BOOKS BY DR. SARAH MORGAN

1. 7 Days of Fasting and Prayer
2. 21 Days of Fasting and Prayer
3. 30 Days of Fasting and Prayer
4. Confessing the Proverbs
5. Declaring the Psalms
6. Intercession by Pattern
7. Prayer the Master Key Revised Edition
8. Sing O' Barren Revised Edition
9. Seed of a Women
10. The Prayer Factor
11. The Faith Factor
12. You Shall Decree a Thing

To Sponsor a Prayer Academy Seminar in your city, to invite Sarah Morgan to your next conference, service, encounter, Revival, Crusade, or for additional information, please contact the Prayer Academy administrative offices.

To enroll or for additional information regarding **Prayer Academy University (PAU),** please visit www.prayeracademy.university

Contact Information:
Email: admin@prayeracademyglobal.com
Phone: 1-888-320-5622 ext.1

ABOUT THE AUTHOR

SARAH MORGAN is skillful, prolific, insightful, and balanced in the teaching of God's word and mightily used in the gifts of the Holy Spirit. Sarah Morgan is an anointed and appointed vessel of God who has shaken the community of Los Angeles and abroad. She has been honored with several awards that recognize her contributions to the community, influence in leadership, and examples of accomplishments and sacrifice for family and friends. She is the Chancellor of Prayer Academy University, and she facilitates Prayer Academy Seminars, conferences, and retreats, which serve to equip, empower and transform ministry leaders from "Doctrine to Demonstration" with the mandate to preserve the Legacy of Prayer in the church.

Sarah Morgan's ministry is sought after and has taken her to South, East and West Africa, London, and across the United States. Everywhere she goes, the power of God within her is demonstrated as the atmosphere changes in her presence, and forces in existence move back to accommodate the Word of God.